John
Glenn

John Glenn

Astronaut and U.S. Senator

ROBERT GREEN

Ferguson Publishing Company
Chicago, Illinois

Photographs ©: AP/Wideworld: 53, 59, 81, 91; Archive Photos: 12, 26, 28, 33, 39, 65, 66, 71, 78, 98; Corbis: 8, 16, 22, 41, 51, 62, 68, 74, 83; Liaison Agency: 10, 60, 87, 89, 94, 96–97, 100

An Editorial Directions Book

Library of Congress Cataloging-in-Publication Data
Green, Robert, 1969–
    John Glenn : astronaut and U.S. senator / by Robert Green.
    p. cm. — (Ferguson's career biographies)
    Includes bibliographical references and index.
    ISBN 0-89434-341-6
    1. Glenn, John, 1921—Juvenile literature. 2. Astronauts—United States—Biogra-
phy—Juvenile literature. 3. United States. Congress. Senate—Biography—Juvenile literature. 4. Legislators—United States—Biography—Juvenile literature. [1. Glenn, John,
1921–. 2. Astronauts. 3. Legislators.] I. Title. II. Series.

TL789.85G6 G74 2000
629.45'0092—dc21
[B]   00-039368

Copyright © 2000 by Ferguson Publishing Company
Published and distributed by
Ferguson Publishing Company
200 West Jackson Boulevard, Suite 700
Chicago, Illinois 60606
www.fergpubco.com

Printed in the United States of America
X-8

CONTENTS

"ZERO G, AND I FEEL FINE"

N THE EARLY MORNING HOURS of February 20, 1962, John Herschel Glenn Jr., clad in a silver space suit and a fishbowl helmet, rode an elevator to the top of the most powerful rocket ever built. As the sun struggled to break through the clouds, spectators gathered on the beaches around Florida's Cape Canaveral Air Station. From Cocoa Beach, they had a clear view across the water to the Cape. They stood by their two-tone, tail-finned automobiles, painted in all the colors of gumdrops. These roomy steel autos were a testament to America's love of speed,

John Glenn on his way to the Atlas rocket that would take him into space to orbit Earth. The mission was successful on February 20, 1962.

mobility, and riches. These Americans joined the millions of television viewers watching the greatest journey ever known—a flight out of this world.

The 125-ton Atlas rocket would fire Glenn through Earth's atmosphere like a human cannon-ball. This was the eleventh time Glenn had climbed into the tiny capsule at the top of the rocket. He had gone through the long preflight routine ten times before. He had slurped down a light breakfast, tested his suit to make sure it didn't leak, and made a last call to Annie, his wife. On this eleventh try, a bolt in the hatch broke and the headset arm snapped off. After everything was fixed, the gantry—the scaffold used to reach the capsule—was pulled back. Glenn called Annie again.

"Hey, Honey," he said, "don't be scared. Remember, I'm just going down to the corner store to get a pack of gum."

"Don't be long," she said.

Countdown

The countdown began. Glenn was sitting on top of thousands of pounds of quick-burning rocket fuel. Suddenly, the rocket ignited, releasing white billows of exhaust smoke. "Pipes whined and creaked below

Glenn, remembering the Atlas rocket liftoff, said, "Pipes whined and creaked below me."

me," Glenn remembered. "The booster shook and thumped when the crew gimbaled the engines. I was clearly sitting on a huge, complex machine. We had joked that we were riding into space on a collection of parts supplied by the lowest bidder on a government contract, and I could hear all of them."

At 9:47 A.M., the countdown reached zero and the giant rocket shuddered off the launchpad. Fire blazed from underneath. The control station was lost in a haze of smoke. Scott Carpenter, another astronaut in the U.S. space program, radioed a parting message: "Godspeed, John Glenn." But Glenn heard only the rattle of the engines as his body shook violently.

The rocket's fuel tanks burned in stages and were released automatically. As these booster rockets fell away, the remaining lighter rocket went even faster, reaching a top speed of 17,545 miles (28,000 kilometers) per hour. Glenn had to struggle against the crushing G-force created by the Earth's gravitational pull, which threatened to shake the rocket into a million pieces.

Five minutes into the flight, John Glenn became the third American to escape Earth's atmosphere. The pressure stopped, and the astronaut found him-

Glenn was taken by the beauty of the planet and enjoyed watching sunrises and sunsets.

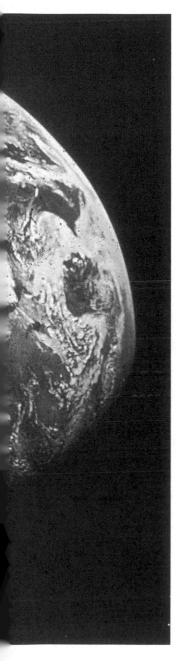

self in the silence of the heavens. "Zero G, and I feel fine," he reported to Canaveral. Glenn floated in the gravity-free space capsule, which he had named *Friendship 7*.

Touring Earth

As the capsule turned onto its side to begin orbiting, Earth came into view, glowing green and blue. "Oh, that view is tremendous," he said. The spacecraft orbited Earth in an eastward direction.

Glenn released himself from his harness and drifted around the capsule, working the instrument panels and performing the many tasks required of an astronaut. He gave himself an eye test because some of his doctors feared that the shape of the eyeball might change in zero gravity, distorting the astronaut's vision. But his vision was fine.

Seven minutes into orbit, Glenn was over Africa. People he could talk to, called Capcoms (Capsule Communications), had been set up in stations around the globe. Glenn radioed the Canary Islands Capcom. "Have a beautiful view of the African coast," he reported. As he sped eastward, he glimpsed a massive sandstorm in the Sahara. The world sped by beneath him.

As he crossed the Indian Ocean, Glenn caught sight of a dark shadow approaching quickly. His spacecraft had been traveling so quickly that he had caught up with nightfall.

Sunrises and sunsets had always left an impression on Glenn. He found them more beautiful than any human art. He had been looking forward to seeing one of these natural displays from space.

"It was even more spectacular than I imagined," he later wrote. "From my orbiting front porch, the setting sun that would have lingered during a long earthly twilight sank eighteen times as fast. The sun was fully round and as white as a brilliant arc light, and then it swiftly disappeared and seemed to melt into a long thin line of rainbow-brilliant radiance along the curve of the horizon."

As he crossed into the deep night of space, Glenn

switched on the lights embedded in the fingertips of his gloves and worked the controls. "That was the shortest day I've ever run into," he radioed to the Australian Capcom station. Glenn became the first person in the world to see the sun rise and set four times in a single day, as *Friendship 7* orbited the Earth.

New Concord

There was something about John Glenn and his adventure that appealed to not only people in the United States, but also to people around the world. Associated Press reporter Saul Pett guessed that it was Glenn's easy manner.

"In the saddle of success," Pett wrote, "he rode loose and easy, and everyone found something to like." People liked Glenn because he meant what he said, spoke easily, and liked to joke around. He had, in short, the old-fashioned virtues of small-town America, which he had learned while growing up in New Concord, Ohio.

John Herschel Glenn Jr. was born on July 18, 1921, in the town of Cambridge, Ohio, just a few miles from New Concord. He had the reddish hair of his mother, Clara Sproat Glenn. His father John Her-

John Hershel Glenn Jr. at the age of four months. He was known as "Bud" throughout his youth.

schel Glenn Sr. was usually called Herschel, but to avoid confusion the son was nicknamed "Bud."

When Bud was two years old, Herschel entered into a partnership with a plumber in New Concord and opened a plumbing supply store on the town's main street. Clara had given up teaching after her son was born and now she watched the shop while Herschel was out fixing pipes. The shop became Bud's playpen. He fidgeted with the parts on the shelves and crawled around on the wooden floor. Later, he was joined by a sister, Jean, whom his parents adopted.

The Glenns' home in New Concord overlooked U.S. Route 40, the main road from Baltimore to St. Louis, and freight and passenger trains of the B & O Railroad cruised by on the tracks next to the highway. The trains gave Glenn the feeling that there was a much larger world outside waiting to be discovered.

Wars Past

Life in New Concord revolved around the three Presbyterian churches and Muskingum College. One of the deepest impressions New Concord left on young John Glenn was its patriotism. "Love of country was a given," wrote Glenn. "Defense of its ideals was an obligation."

Herschel Glenn had served in France after the United States entered World War I in 1917. And though he returned partly deaf from the explosion of an artillery shell, Herschel was a proud veteran.

On the Fourth of July and Memorial Day, Herschel marched through New Concord with the Thirty-Seventh Ohio Division. He played his army bugle in the holiday parades and for the flag-raising ceremonies.

Glenn idolized his father and took up the trumpet so that he could learn to play along with him. After Bud had learned the basics of playing the trumpet, his father asked him to play for a Memorial Day service. Bud practiced for hours to master each note of taps, the traditional lament for fallen soldiers.

By Memorial Day, Bud finally had it down. Following the three-volley salute of the honor guard, his father started to play. "The first sad notes rose in the spring air," Glenn wrote. "I put the trumpet to my lips and echoed the clear notes. We played through taps like that, my trumpet echoing his bugle phrase by phrase, until the last notes died. Echo taps still gives me the chills," Glenn wrote nearly seven decades later.

First Flight

The summer that John Glenn turned eight, his father introduced him to what would become one of the great passions of his life—flying. Driving by a grass airstrip in the rolling hill country of Ohio, Herschel Glenn stopped his car so that his son could take a look at an old biplane. "Do you want to go up, Bud?" his father asked.

Of course, he already knew the answer. Bud thought it was the greatest thing that could ever happen to him.

Bud squeezed into the back cockpit with his father, and the pilot worked the controls from the front cockpit. The engine grew louder as the plane picked up speed over the bumpy grass runway. Suddenly, Bud was soaring off Earth's surface for the first time in his life. He strained to see out over the edge of the cockpit and watch the ground below. He could see for miles and imagined how birds must feel in flight. "I was hooked on flying after that," Glenn wrote, "on the idea of swooping and soaring."

Bud never forgot that sense of freedom, the

excitement and wonder of soaring above Earth. At school, he had been taught about Orville and Wilbur Wright of Dayton, Ohio, who had flown the first heavier-than-air machine in 1903. The Wright brothers had given the people of Ohio a personal pride in the development of aviation.

After his first flight, Bud added building model airplanes to his list of hobbies. His parents bought him slim boxes of balsa-wood cutouts, from which he constructed different types of flying machines.

Bud's other hobbies included fishing in nearby Crooked Creek, hunting, and the activities of the Rangers. The Rangers was a club that Glenn and some other boys had started to emulate the Boy Scouts. The Rangers lived by the code of the Boy Scouts and tried to be brave and honorable.

Growing Up in Hard Times

Bud had a happy, industrious childhood despite his parents' lack of money. By 1933, millions of people had lost their jobs. Many families also lost their savings and were forced to sell their homes. Migrant workers drifted across the country searching for work. This tragic time in the country's history is known as the Great Depression, the longest, most difficult period of poverty ever known in the United States.

Bud's parents were fortunate during those years. Although money was tight, his father continued to work, and the people of New Concord pulled together to help each other out. Bud worked in the family garden, and often took extra vegetables to other families. He also hawked tickets at the downtown movie house, sold stalks of rhubarb door to door, and hunted rabbits with the rifle his father had given him. The Glenn family weathered the Great Depression successfully, and Bud grew into a broad-faced, sturdy young man who was much respected around New Concord.

As Glenn entered high school, his interests were starting to turn in another direction. He continued to play football. He also still hung around with his old friends from the Rangers, but he was beginning to spend more and more time with a girl named Annie Castor, whom he had already been friends with for many years.

As a baby, Bud played with Annie while their parents played cards. So, from earliest memory, Annie had been a part of Bud's life.

"The things we did as part of a group—the ice-

Young John Glenn with his longtime girlfriend, Annie Castor.
The two were married in 1943.

cream socials and the cookouts, the swimming and ice skating at College Lake—continued, but we routinely paired off now. We were a couple. I had always liked Annie's smile. It revealed all the warmth and eagerness that was there, though hidden to some by the difficulty she had speaking. Now her smile struck me in a different way. I started to look forward to that feeling."

FIGHTING BIRDMAN

2

THE YEAR BEFORE Glenn graduated from high school, Annie turned down a music scholarship to study at the Juilliard School in New York City. The promising organist chose to remain in New Concord instead. She enrolled one year ahead of Glenn at Muskingum College. The young couple had already discussed marriage, even considered an elopement, but they decided to wait and see what the future would bring.

The world outside New Concord was changing quickly. In 1939, John Glenn

President Franklin Delano Roosevelt wished to keep the United States out of World War II, but that proved impossible.

enrolled in Muskingum to major in chemistry. The same year, war broke out in Europe. Bud read about the German army's invasion of France in the local papers. Here was war again on the same battlefields that his father had fought on two decades earlier. The war was still far off, but John Glenn shared the feeling that the United States could easily be drawn into the conflict.

President Franklin Delano Roosevelt pledged to keep the United States out of the war, but many Americans wanted desperately to help America's allies in Europe. For two years, Roosevelt resisted the persuasion of British Prime Minister Winston Churchill, who wanted the U.S. Army to help fight the Nazis in Europe.

As Adolf Hitler's army stamped out resistance in Europe during the early days of World War II, Great Britain itself was threatened. The Luftwaffe—the German air force—bombed London and other British cities. Hitler hoped to force Britain to surrender and threatened full-scale invasion of the island nation.

From the summer of 1940 to the spring of 1941, Glenn read about the Luftwaffe's attacks on Britain and followed dramatic radio broadcasts from Lon-

Prime Minister Winston Churchill of Great Britain hoped to gain American support in the war.

don. By the summer of 1941, the British Royal Air Force (RAF) had fended off the attack of the overwhelmingly superior numbers of German aircraft.

The RAF pilots alone had saved Great Britain from collapse. "Never in the field of human conflict was so much owed by so many to so few," said Churchill about the RAF pilots.

When Glenn came across an advertisement for a pilot-training program the following semester, he enrolled immediately. Glenn trained on a Taylor-craft, a two-seater airplane with a closed canopy. The plane could reach only 80 to 90 miles (129 to 145 kilometers) per hour, but that was enough for the new pilot. After some classroom work, Glenn learned to taxi the plane and to take the controls from the pilot once they were in the air. "I loved it," he wrote. "The total attention that flying demanded was exhilarating. I felt when I was in the air that all my senses were operating at their fullest."

After hours of flight time and countless nerve-racking takeoffs and landings, Glenn flew his first solo flight. His instructor gave him no warning, but just told him to take the Taylorcraft around the landing strip and bring it back in on his own. For the first time in his life, Glenn faced the skies by himself. "It was easier than it would have been if I'd had advance warning," Glenn wrote. About a month before his twenty-first birthday, John Glenn was awarded his pilot's license. The new pilot celebrated by taking his father up for a ride.

Called to Battle

On December 7, 1941, John Glenn was driving toward Muskingum campus to hear Annie perform an organ recital. The announcer interrupted the radio program with the shocking news that the Japanese had attacked Pearl Harbor, Hawaii. Glenn knew that the United States might enter the war at any time. Nobody had expected the treacherous surprise attack that left U.S. warships burning in Pearl Harbor that Sunday morning.

After the recital, Glenn and Annie stayed up nearly all night. "I have to go," Glenn said. He was determined to follow in his father's footsteps and enlist. Americans could no longer talk of staying out of the war. The Japanese had delivered the first punch. President Roosevelt declared war on Japan the day after the attack. Japan's allies—Germany and Italy—then declared war on the United States. The United States suddenly found itself in a conflict that stretched around the globe.

Glenn enlisted in the Army Air Corps and waited for orders. By the following spring—March 1942—

orders still hadn't arrived. He re-enlisted, this time in the Naval Aviation Cadet Program. "I wasn't sure that I might not be AWOL [absent without leave] from the Army, but I made plans to go."

Orders from the Navy came quickly. His first stop was the Naval Aviation Pre-Flight School in Iowa City, Iowa. Glenn left Muskingum before finishing his degree, and now he was thrown into a combination of difficult classes as well as military training. He learned about aeronautics, navigation, military history, and how to identify enemy aircraft. When they weren't in class, Glenn and the other cadets played football, boxed, and performed rigorous physical training.

The real fun began once the basic training was over. Glenn reported to a naval base at Olathe, Kansas. The pilots trained on Stearman biplanes. These planes were more powerful than the Taylorcraft Glenn had learned to fly, but not much like the fighters they would soon fly in the war. The Stearmans looked more like World War I surplus. Nevertheless, Glenn was happy to be back in the cockpit. He had the advantage of already having a pilot's license, and he was soon looping and diving in combat-simulation exercises. Glenn developed a knack for the controls and felt comfortable in the air. "I began to develop the sense that Wally Spotts back in the Civilian Pilot Training Program had called the kinesthetics of flying—a feeling that the plane was an extension of myself. My hands moved on the controls without my having to think about it, and the plane responded to my thought."

The training station in Olathe was short one essential person—it didn't have a bugler! When word got out that Glenn could sound the calls, he added the daily rituals of morning reveille and nighttime taps to his duties. Just as his father had done, Glenn began and ended the day with his horn. Military life suited Glenn. He liked the camaraderie of the men and the constant challenges.

Glenn wrote to Annie nearly every day and visited her when he had leave, but it became harder to see her once he was transferred to the Navy flight school in Corpus Christi, Texas. While he learned to fly more-advanced aircraft, Annie worked as a secretary for a colonel in the Army Air Corps.

Glenn put in for a commission with the Marines when he finished his advanced training at Corpus Christi in March 1943. Once he had reached the rank of second lieutenant, the Marines allowed him

Glenn was musically inclined. Playing the bugle was one of his military responsibilities.

to get married. If there was one thing that Second Lieutenant Glenn was more eager for than combat, it was to see Annie. The two were married at a Presbyterian church in New Dayton, Ohio, on April 6, 1943. John Glenn had left New Dayton eager to prove himself in the world, and now he had returned in his blue uniform and white Marine's cap to marry his hometown sweetheart. "There was never a time when we didn't know each other. I married my friend," Glenn later said.

Island-Hopping

As Glenn honeymooned with Annie, the war raged on in the Pacific. Japan had spread its soldiers across Asia in the early days of the war. They secured a strip of coast on the Chinese mainland, quickly seized Vietnam, Cambodia, Thailand, Burma, and Indonesia, and drove the Americans out of the Philippines. The Japanese also occupied most of the craggy, volcanic islands of the Pacific Ocean.

The U.S. Navy regrouped, and after the Pearl Harbor attack, American factories pumped out war supplies in undreamed-of quantities. When the men shipped out to war, their wives, mothers, and sisters took factory jobs. Soon, the United States was fighting the Japanese in battles staged on the sea, in the air, and on land battles. In the Pacific, the American strategy was to move from island to island. Islands that were too strongly fortified were passed by, but were left without supplies from the Japanese navy. This military strategy was called island-hopping.

Marines did much of the fighting in the island-hopping campaign. Many men were killed on the barren outposts that dotted the Pacific. Japanese soldiers were under orders not to surrender. Many fought to the death in heavily fortified rocks and caves on the islands. If the enemy's positions proved too strong for the U.S. ground forces, Marine planes were called in to swoop down and bomb the Japanese. Second Lieutenant Glenn trained rigorously for aerial combat and bombing runs at the Marine Air Station at El Centro, California, which was just across the border from Mexico.

Glenn trained on F4F Wildcats, the first real fighter planes he had flown. The Wildcat was slightly slower than the Japanese Zero, but more heavily armed. To practice flying and shooting at the same time, the pilots closed and fired on a friendly plane towing a long banner. Needless to say, it was a dangerous job for the pilot flying the plane that was towing the target—especially because the shooting pilot had to aim ahead of the mark so that the bullets and the target would be at the same place at the same time. This was called "leading the target."

As the pilot closed in on his target, he aimed through a glass plate in the windshield and measured the distance by a series of marks that circled the sight. "Sighting in and squeezing the trigger as you rushed at the target at 350 miles [565 km] an hour was a thrill," Glenn wrote. "Every third round was a tracer round, so you could see if you were hitting and correct your lead if you weren't."

Glenn trained six days a week at El Centro. The heat of the desert town was unbearable in summer. When there was nothing better to do, air crews cracked eggs on the runways and watched them fry. At home, to provide relief from the heat, Glenn relied on a swamp cooler, a fan that cooled the air by blowing it through a wall of dripping water. Outside the couple's apartment, swarms of crickets made it seem as though the ground was moving. "It was like one of the plagues of Egypt," he wrote. "Driving over their bodies on the road sounded like a bowl of Rice Krispies when you pour in the milk."

In January 1944, after two and a half years of

waiting, Glenn shipped out with his squadron for combat duty in the Pacific. Annie drove their car back to New Dayton while her husband headed out to meet the Japanese.

Glenn met them sooner than he thought. In Hawaii, he was startled to see Japanese Americans everywhere, "running around loose on the streets." He had never been around large groups of Japanese before, but he soon realized these Japanese people were loyal Americans and not the enemy he had been sent to fight.

From Hawaii, Glenn's squadron sailed 2,000 miles (3,200 km) southwest to the Marshall Islands, where Glenn finally came within striking distance of the real Japanese enemy. The Marshalls had already been cut off from the Japanese navy, but many islands were still heavily fortified.

Glenn's first target was the island of Taroa, in the Maloelap Atoll. His squadron was ordered to destroy the gun positions on the island, which were threatening Allied planes. Glenn, leading a squad of four "fighting birdmen," as one journalist dubbed the Marine aviators, strafed [machine-gunned] the island. The strafing runs were designed to protect the American bombers that were screeching down with their deadly payloads by driving the Japanese behind their fortifications.

Diving into fortified enemy positions was extremely dangerous and, when the attack began, the Japanese guns opened up. As the sky filled with bursts of black smoke and lethal fragments of anti-aircraft fire, Glenn nosed downward over the island and fired his 50-caliber guns. "I hit several targets as I came across the island from the south," Glenn remembered. "Streams of tracer fire came at us from the ground. I pulled out very low on the treetops and banked east, and climbed to the rendezvous point."

Glenn had survived his first dive into enemy fire. One of his comrades and closest friends was not so lucky. When Glenn returned to the base at Majuro Island, the reality of war hit him when he saw the empty locker of his friend. "I had never felt so helpless," he wrote. "The pent-up feelings of the last few hours let loose, and I stood there and sobbed."

The pilots received a morale boost when Colonel Charles Lindbergh visited them on the island of Majuro. Lindbergh had made aviation history in 1927 when he became the first man to complete a nonstop solo flight across the Atlantic Ocean. He navigated his tiny plane, the *Spirit of St. Louis*, from

Pilot Charles Lindbergh and his plane the Spirit of St. Louis. *The famous aviator's visit to Glenn's Marine squadron was a welcome event.*

New York to Paris in less than thirty-four hours. Lindbergh's flight had made him a national hero and John Glenn's personal hero. Although Lindbergh had been against the war, he had enlisted as a flight instructor after the attack on Pearl Harbor. Lindbergh lived with the aviators in their homemade coconut-log huts and swam in the crystal blue waters of the Pacific. The Marines were glad to have him with them.

Glenn's squadron was moved west, closer to Japan. On Tarawa Atoll, Glenn got a view of the devastation left by earlier ground fighting. The Marines had fought for the island for three days and nights. In the end, only 17 Japanese survived out of a force of 5,000. Glenn was impressed with the fanatical bravery that the Japanese had shown in fending off the Allied attacks.

As the Allies closed in on the Japanese home islands in 1945, resistance stiffened. Japan and its home islands became a fortress of Japanese soldiers willing to die for their emperor.

After flying fifty-nine missions in the Pacific and being hit by antiaircraft fire five times, John Glenn received orders to return to the United States for leave. The news was welcome indeed. Although he had acted courageously, earning two Distinguished Flying Crosses and ten Air Medals, Glenn now looked forward to seeing Annie and living quietly for a few weeks.

Fighting in the Pacific continued. In March 1945, General Douglas MacArthur landed in the Philip-

General Douglas MacArthur (left) with soldiers in the Philippines. His capture of the islands was a triumph for the Allied forces.

pine Islands, which he had famously promised to return to after being driven out by the Japanese in 1941. "Hoist the colors and let no enemy ever haul them down," he said. The capture of the Philippines allowed the Allies to focus on invading the Japanese home islands. Glenn assumed that his squadron would be part of the invasion of Japan. But the Allied leaders realized that invading Japan would cost many Allied lives. America decided to use its new secret weapon against two Japanese targets.

At 9:15 the morning of August 6, 1945, the city of Hiroshima disappeared in a flash of radioactive light caused by a single atomic bomb. Three days later, Nagasaki, an industrial city that produced war materials for Japan's navy, suffered the same fate. Nobody had ever seen anything as powerful and frightening as these new weapons. On August 14, Emperor Hirohito addressed the Japanese people in his first-ever radio address. He announced that Japan had completely surrendered. Germany had surrendered on May 7, 1945. The United States was at peace for the first time in five years.

SPEED DEMON

THE END OF THE WAR left Glenn wondering what to do about his career. His father tried to convince him to join his plumbing business, but Glenn was too excited about flying, especially in combat. "The danger of combat flying did nothing to diminish my love of flying in general. If anything, it enhanced it. This was flying with a purpose." In 1945, Captain John Glenn accepted a commission with the Marine Corps. He was now a professional combat pilot.

Annie gave birth to their first child, David, that same year. Glenn, who had always looked up to his father, now had his own son. In 1947, Annie gave birth to a girl, Carolyn, whom they always called Lyn. The family moved to the Marine base in Guam, an island in the Pacific. The Chinese Civil War, which had begun before World War II, had simmered throughout the global war. After 1945, the two sides in the conflict—the Communists and the Nationalists leapt at one another's throats.

Cold War

Glenn was assigned bombing missions over China, where the U.S. military was helping its wartime ally, the Nationalist Party. In the end, however, the Communists under Mao Zedong proved to be more popular with the people. In 1949, the Nationalist Party fled to the island of Taiwan and formed an independent government. In Beijing, Mao proclaimed the founding of the People's Republic of China.

The United States had become increasingly concerned about the spread of Communism. The Soviet Union, a wartime ally, wanted to spread the Communist revolution worldwide. Communist beliefs were contrary to everything that America believed in: democracy, capitalism, and the rule of law. The

United States began a massive arms buildup, preparing to fight the Communists. The arms race sparked a new kind of war called the Cold War.

The United States and the Soviet Union tried to out-maneuver each other and threatened to destroy each other with their massive arsenals. Sometimes, small wars broke out in nations where the Soviets and the Americans were both trying to promote their way of life. One such war was fought in Korea.

"MiG Mad Marine"

The Korean peninsula was divided into two countries in 1948. The North Koreans, with Soviet help and encouraged by the Communist victory in China, had a Communist government. The South Koreans turned to the international community for support in keeping the Communists out. The United Nations (UN) sent an international group of soldiers to South Korea. When war broke out in 1950, some thought it could be the beginning of another world war.

John Glenn followed the outbreak of the Korean War from a Marine training base on the island of Guadalcanal. He itched to get into the fight—not only to fly combat missions again, but because he believed in fighting Communism. "The Communist government in Russia wants to control all the countries right now," he wrote in a letter to his daughter. "If we let them do it, it might mean that they wouldn't let us live where we wanted to live, you and Dave couldn't go to school where you could learn what you should, and they would take a lot of the things we have now." Glenn requested a transfer to Korea.

In October 1952, his request was granted, and he joined the U.N. forces in the numbing cold of the Korean winter. The planes that the Marines were flying were Panther jets. More than twenty years after his first ride in a prop-driven biplane, Glenn now navigated a flying propeller-free rocket. He loved every minute of it.

His squad flew many missions well behind enemy lines, similar to the strafing runs he made in the Pacific. Glenn destroyed gun emplacements, bridges, and ammunition depots. The greatest danger, as in the Pacific, was the enemy antiaircraft.

The Koreans lured pilots down to seemingly isolated targets and then opened up with flak guns from surrounding positions. Once the pilot dived on the target, it was too late to pull up, and the sky would fill with thousands of antiaircraft rounds.

Glenn experienced this firsthand on a bombing run near Sinanju. As he dived toward a target, he saw the flashing of a gun emplacement below. After releasing his bombs, he swooped around toward the new target, flying just above the trees. "I flew fast and low directly at the gun emplacement, firing the four 20-mm cannons, and watched the shells tear that emplacement to pieces," he wrote. "That was solid satisfaction."

As he pulled up, he heard a deafening thud, and his plane nearly veered into the ground. At 500 miles (800 km) per hour, he struggled with the controls and missed hitting a ridge by what seemed like inches. All around him, the sky filled with antiaircraft fire. Somehow he flew his plane home. A picture of Glenn safely back at the base shows a cocky flyboy with a wide grin, standing next to the tail of his aircraft. The sun shines through a hole about the size of a man's head in the tail fin of the Panther jet. "My closest call," the caption reads.

Glenn longed for one last adventure in combat flying, a dogfight. He had never before encountered enemy aircraft. He knew a Marine flier was supposed to support ground troops and leave the enemy aircraft to the Air Force. Glenn was accepted for a transfer on a pilot-exchange program to fly for the U.S. Air Force.

His assignment was to patrol the Yalu River, which separates North Korea and China. Russian-made MiG fighter planes screeched across the border regularly to pound UN troops and shoot down aircraft. Glenn was afraid that the war might end before he had the chance to meet a MiG in the air. His enthusiasm made such an impression on his flight team that they had "MiG Mad Marine" painted on the side of his jet.

Glenn finally got his chance at aerial combat while leading a four-plane patrol over North Korea. Flying at 43,000 thousand feet (13,000 meters), he spotted the sleek, silvery outline of a MiG in the distance. "I kept after him at seven hundred miles per hour, gaining very slowly," he recalled. "I finally caught him forty miles inside Manchuria."

Glenn opened fire in Chinese airspace, and his bullets ripped through the MiG. "I was only fifty feet off the ground, and I flew through a cloud of his debris to find myself looking right down the runway of a Chinese air base." Glenn fired a few bursts at the control tower, shattering the glass windows, and then headed for home. He had finally got his MiG.

Glenn painted a red star under the canopy of the cockpit to indicate he had downed an enemy plane. Two more red stars would join the first one in the next couple of months. The pilot had finally learned the dangerous ballet of dogfighting.

In July 1953, peace between North and South Korea was restored. John Glenn returned to the United States.

Project Bullet

Being a combat pilot meant maneuvering the plane while the enemy was firing. It required dedication to the plane, to the preflight checks, and to the training that honed a pilot's skills.

Glenn personified these traits. His easy smile, humility, and common sense were only some of the man's qualities. Another was his sheer madness—his willingness to tempt death just to see how good a pilot he was. Glenn was a perfect example of the fighter pilot. He had a sense of his own mortality on the ground, but once aloft, he became a demon of the skies. After the war, he settled for the most dangerous job in peacetime flying. He became a military test pilot.

Glenn went to the Naval Air Test Center at Maryland's Patuxent River National Air Station. Once again, he scratched his head at complex physics problems, trying to keep up with students who had done little or no combat flying. He struggled through classes, longing for the flying to begin.

American aviation technology jumped forward in the years after World War II. Glenn experienced this technological progress in the Chance Vought F8U Crusader, a new supersonic jet fighter. The plane had a top speed of 1,015 miles (1,630 km) per hour. It was the fastest navy fighter in the world.

The risk of flying the Crusader was constantly driven home to the pilots as their comrades died in fiery wrecks and midair breakups. But Glenn could not fly the jets and think about danger at the same time. He chose only to fly.

His goal was to break the cross-country speed record in the Crusader. The project, which Glenn named Project Bullet, because he would have to fly faster than a bullet fired from a .45 pistol, took nearly two years of intense lobbying. The plane had already shown incredible speed and maneuverability, and the Pentagon and Navy Command had to be persuaded to let Glenn top the record. The cost of the project would be enormous.

John Glenn with his family after he broke the cross-country speed record on July 16, 1957

Finally, Project Bullet was approved. Major John H. Glenn boarded the Crusader on the overcast morning of July 16, 1957. Glenn screeched off the runway and burst through the cloud cover in seconds, climbing to 51,000 thousand feet (15,548 m). His average speed was more than 1,000 miles (1,600 km) per hour, faster than the speed of sound.

Only three times on the 2,455-mile (3,955 km) flight from California to New York would Glenn ease off the thrusters. Because the plane burned fuel so quickly, he had to perform a complicated link with a midair refueling plane high above New Mexico, Kansas, and Indiana.

On the flight, he passed within a few miles of New Concord, where his parents, friends, and neighbors were watching from the ground. As he screamed overhead, the plane's supersonic speed caused sonic booms by breaking the sound barrier. The booms rattled the town, and one of Glenn's neighbors ran to the Glenns' house screaming, "Mrs. Glenn, Johnny dropped a bomb! Johnny dropped a bomb!" Most Americans had never heard of a sonic boom and had no idea what it was.

When Glenn landed at Floyd Bennett Field on Long Island, New York, he learned that he had

Secretary of the Navy Thomas Gates (left) presents Glenn with the Distinguished Flying Cross.

crossed the country in 3 hours, 23 minutes, and 8.4 seconds, beating the previous record by 21 minutes.

Glenn was greeted on the ground by the flash of newsmen's cameras and a military band playing "Anchors Away" and the "Marine Hymn." Glenn was worried about Annie. He knew the press would want to interview her and that her stutter would make this difficult. "I had a pang of conscience that stepping into the spotlight like this might not be fair to her," he wrote.

But John Glenn's day in the sun had just begun. He was asked for dozens of interviews and appeared on the popular TV show *Name That Tune* in his khaki uniform. America loved a hero. John Glenn was just getting started, for there was a new project on the horizon—a mission that would make "John Glenn" a household name.

SPACE RACE

URING THE COLD WAR, both the Americans and the Soviets were spending millions and millions of dollars on the race to put a man in space. It was a competition on the grandest scale.

Some Americans criticized plans to put a man in space as a waste of time and said it was undertaken just because of national pride. But there was a more threatening aspect to the Soviet and American desire to control the heavens. Rockets used to launch space flights were the same rockets used to carry nuclear warheads. The Soviets had discovered the secret to building nuclear weapons shortly after World War II. By the time of the space race, both countries had built nuclear warheads that would dwarf the explosions that had occurred at Hiroshima and Nagasaki.

People were afraid that one of these countries would learn to launch weapons from orbit. The space programs of the Soviet Union and the United States brought both countries closer, not only to perfecting long-range rockets, but to military domination of the world.

To beat the Soviets into space, U.S. President Dwight D. Eisenhower established the National Aeronautics and Space Administration (NASA). But the "godless Communists," as Glenn called the Soviets, struck first. On October 4, 1957, they launched the world's first artificial satellite, *Sputnik*, into orbit. Americans stood by helplessly as *Sputnik* orbited the globe.

In the U.S. Congress, criticism rang out sharply. "The Roman Empire controlled the world because it could build roads," said Senator Lyndon Johnson of Texas in response to the Soviet triumph. "Later, when it moved to sea, the British Empire was dominant because it had ships. In the air age, we were powerful because we had airplanes. Now the Communists have established a foothold in outer space."

Project Mercury

To counter the Soviets, NASA unveiled Project Mercury, which it said would put an American citizen in space. To find recruits to man space flights, NASA opened a competition to the armed services to find the first group of America's new breed of warrior-explorer—the astronaut.

The uncertainty and danger of space flight intrigued Glenn, who was bored with his desk job at a military research center in Langley, Virginia. "I volunteered without hesitation," Glenn recalled.

The process of choosing the first group of astronauts was difficult. Of the 508 original candidates accepted on the basis of experience, education, and size, only seven made the final cut. NASA subjected the candidates to every form of mental and physical testing that they could think of. These candidates suffered through a series of grueling physical fitness tests that determined just how much their hearts and lungs could take. When their bodies were nearly broken, the psychological tests began, to give NASA a view into how the men's minds worked.

The tests would have driven any normal person insane—and they were meant to.

Candidate John Glenn, the examiners discovered, seemed to enjoy the test, however. He went through the steps of each one with a sense of curiosity, however. The tests were designed to confuse the candidates and find their mental and physical breaking points. The men were shaken, stirred, pressurized, and probed—all with the idea of testing their endurance.

NASA was particularly impressed with Glenn's ability to keep calm under pressure. The test known as the Who Am I? test was specifically designed to find out if the candidates possessed rock-solid confidence and a sense of purpose. When he was asked the question, Glenn answered, "I am a man; I am a Marine; I am a flyer; I am an officer; I am a father." This was just the kind of answer that NASA was looking for. Glenn made the final cut.

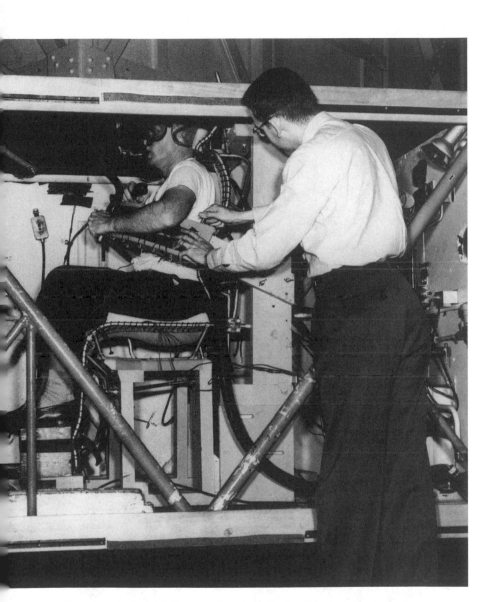

Glenn went through hours of testing during his training to be an astronaut.

The first seven U.S. astronauts. John Glenn is in the front row, second from right. Alan Shepard, the first American in space, is in the back row at far left.

To present the seven exceptional men chosen as the first squad of U.S. astronauts, NASA arranged a press conference in Washington, D.C. When the seven pilots—three of them from the Air Force, three from the Navy, and one from the Marines— took center stage that day, they had no idea what they were in for.

Journalists and photographers packed the room. The lights for the television cameras heated up the entire room and created an uncomfortable hothouse atmosphere. The astronauts blinked, and shuffled their feet, uncertain how to answer the rapid-fire barrage of questions.

The proud Glenn family in 1959 (left to right): daughter, Carolyn; son, David; wife, Annie; and Glenn's parents, Clara and Herschel

Glenn, aged thirty-seven and the oldest of the group, stole the show. His easy charm and guileless grin had come in handy in his earlier stint as an American hero after his Project Bullet cross-country flight.

"I got on this program because it probably would be the nearest to heaven I would ever get," Glenn told the reporters, emerging as the natural spokesman for the group, "and I wanted to make the most of it. . . . This whole project sort of stands with us now like the way the Wright brothers stood at Kitty Hawk fifty years ago, with Orville and Wilbur pitching a coin to see who was going to shove the other one off the hill down there."

From that day on, Glenn was a celebrity. The astronauts signed a contract that gave the exclusive rights to their story to nationally popular weekly *Life* magazine. The purpose of the contract was not to favor this one publication but rather to reduce the number of reporters who were chasing the story. *Life* reporters practically moved in with the astronauts, filming them while they were in their homes, on vacations, and in training.

As the Mercury Project tested rockets, the entire world watched. NASA was a civilian organization from its beginning, despite its close connection with the military, so its activities were open to public scrutiny.

So, the press was on hand when NASA attempted to launch the Vanguard rocket in 1957. NASA hoped the Vanguard would one day carry a man to space. As the rocket ignited on live television, it rumbled up a few feet, with smoke and fire billowing from its base. Suddenly, the rocket began to collapse, and the fuel tanks exploded in a great ball of orange fire. Soviet Premier Nikita Khrushchev saw the broadcast and afterward sarcastically referred to the satellite that the Vanguard was supposed to launch into space as an "orange."

The Soviets then had another success. On April 12, 1961, twenty-seven-year-old Yuri Gagarin orbited Earth. Not only had the Soviets put a man in space

Russian cosmonaut Yuri Gagarin. On April 12, 1961, he became the first man to orbit Earth.

In 1961, Alan Shepard made history as the first American in space. Glenn would have to wait another year for his chance.

ahead of the Americans, but their cosmonaut (their name for an astronaut) had also orbited—something NASA was not even close to doing.

"Well, they just beat the pants off us, that's all," Glenn said to reporters. "There's no use kidding ourselves about that. Now that the space age has begun, there's going to be plenty of work for everybody."

The Race Continues

Twenty-three days later, the Americans struck back. Many people thought that Glenn would be the first of the seven astronauts to travel into space. Alan Shepard, whom Glenn had voted for in a peer review of the best astronaut, was the first instead. He was launched atop the Atlas rocket in a suborbital flight and returned to Earth as the first American to have traveled in space.

Glenn was assured that he would be able to go next, but again NASA selected one of the other astronauts. Glenn thought that the reason he hadn't been selected might be that he had left college before earning his degree—but whatever the reason, he wanted to be next.

Two weeks later, the Soviet Union launched another man into space. Although the United States

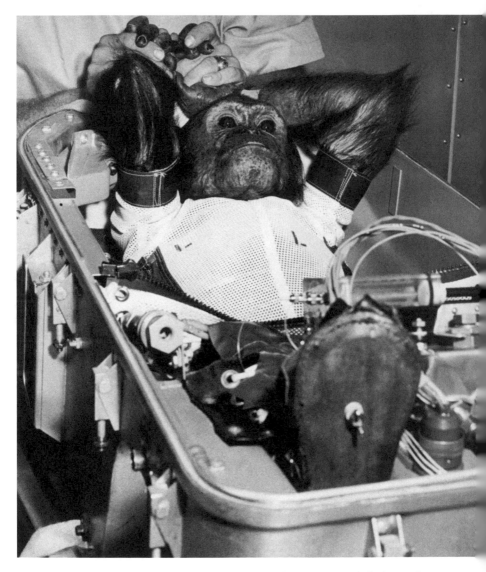

Enos, a chimpanzee, made a successful orbit of Earth before John Glenn gave it a try.

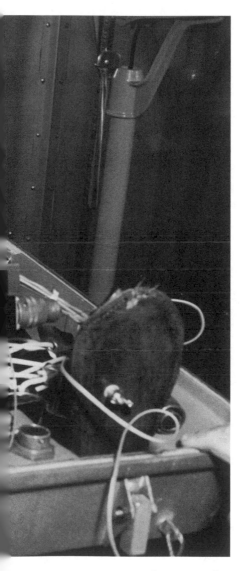

had just managed to fire two astronauts into space, the Soviets now had sent one of its cosmonauts on a flight that orbited Earth seventeen times.

Soon, Glenn received word that he would have a shot at becoming the first American astronaut to orbit Earth. In preparation for Glenn's flight, NASA launched a chimp named Enos in an orbital flight.

After Enos splashed down in the Pacific, he emerged from the capsule and hammed it up for the cameras. Enos's success paved the way for Glenn's mission— although the astronaut was not too happy about the idea of following a chimp into space.

Fall to Earth

When *Friendship 7* blasted off on February 20, 1962, to make its now-famous three orbits around Earth, the mission was far from risk-free, despite Enos's success. On Glenn's third orbit around Earth, a Capcom relayed a disturbing signal to him. A control-panel light had gone on, indicating a problem with the landing bag. Canaveral was worried that the landing bag had shaken loose. If the landing bag had deployed, the heat shield that protected the *Friendship 7* from burning up on reentry would have loosened. Glenn fiddled with his own switches and came up with no problems in the capsule.

Canaveral instructed Glenn to start reentry procedures. Glenn would have to operate some of the functions manually. The retro-rockets, which slowed the capsule and positioned it to reenter the Earth's atmosphere, would normally be discarded on reentry. But Canaveral decided to leave them on until later because they were strapped over the heat shield. If the landing bag had been released, the retro-rockets would help hold the shield in place.

Glenn knew that the heat of reentry would reach 9,500° Fahrenheit (5260° Celsius) and radio communications would be knocked out until he was in

With the Atlas rocket in 1962. John Glenn was eager to face the challenge of space exploration.

Earth's atmosphere. As Glenn received his final communication, he heard a thud beneath the craft. "Flaming pieces of something started streaming past the window," he recalled. "I feared it was the heat shield. Every nerve fiber was attuned to heat along my spine . . . Through the window, I saw the glow intensify to a bright orange. Overhead, the sky was black. The fiery glow wrapped around the capsule, with a circle the color of a lemon drop in the center of its wake."

All three major television networks had camera crews at Cape Canaveral with cameras pointed skyward, and millions of people waited tensely in front of their TV sets. President John F. Kennedy was following the astronaut's progress and prepared to inform the nation of the success or failure of the latest project of the U.S. space program.

Finally, Glenn's voiced crackled over the radio. "Hello, Cape, *Friendship 7*. Do you receive? Over."

"Roger, reading you loud and clear," a relieved Capcom responded. "How are you doing?"

Glenn, out of fuel, was plunging wildly toward Earth. At 28,000 feet (8,500 m), a small parachute released automatically, and at 10,000 feet (3,000 m), the main chute billowed above him. Glenn landed in the Atlantic Ocean just 6 miles (10 km) from the USS *Noa*, which safely hoisted him on board. The heat of reentry had burned off the capsule's American flag and the lettering that read "United States," as if the heavens above were indifferent to the identity of the terrestrial visitor.

President Kennedy addressed the nation: "[Space] is the new ocean, and I believe the United States must sail on it and be in a position second to none." Glenn's mission was not only a new triumph for a much-decorated fighter pilot, but a patriotic victory for the United States. In his almost five-hour flight, Glenn became, for a time, the most celebrated hero of the Cold War. He was honored with a ticker-tape parade 4 million strong in New York and was greeted everywhere he went by the flash of a newsman's camera.

After his space flight, Glenn donated his flight suit, helmet, and a small American flag that he had carried into space to the Smithsonian Institution in Washington, D.C. Later, his space capsule, *Friendship 7*, was installed at the museum as a permanent exhibit. This museum is one of the most visited in the Capital. There could be few honors as great for a pilot as having his craft displayed in that museum,

*Glenn and President John Kennedy (right) inspecting a space
capsule. Kennedy was a strong supporter of the U.S. space
program.*

alongside the Wright brothers' first plane and Charles Lindbergh's *Spirit of St. Louis.*

An American Vision

The young American president, John F. Kennedy, shared in Glenn's triumph. Before Glenn's flight, the president and the astronaut pored over charts and maps and discussed details of the adventure like two generals planning a campaign. Glenn was astounded by all the details of the project that Kennedy had absorbed. The space program fit right into Kennedy's grand vision of American greatness, and he was as swept away by the romanticism of the Space Race as he was by its implications for the Cold War.

After the mission, Kennedy greeted Glenn as a hero. Glenn took to heart Kennedy's challenge to better America. As Kennedy put it in his celebrated 1961 inauguration speech: "Ask not what your country can do for you," he said, "ask what you can do for your country."

While flying on *Air Force One,* the president's official airplane, Glenn was struck by a remark made by Kennedy's daughter, Caroline. Her comment reminded him of how widely publicized the early attempts to reach space had been. The president's wife introduced Glenn to Caroline. "This is the astronaut who went around the Earth in the spaceship," Mrs. Kennedy said. "But where's the monkey?" Caroline asked.

Glenn and Annie were also invited to Hyannis Port, the Massachusetts home of the Kennedy family, to spend time with Robert Kennedy and his wife Ethel. Glenn was always somewhat awed in the company of John Kennedy, but found Robert an easy companion. The two became fast friends.

The Kennedys' vision for the United States clicked with Glenn's. He believed that they shared his deep, unselfish devotion to the United States and to the bravery of its people. The idea of serving the country through politics began to blossom in Glenn's mind, and the Kennedys encouraged him to run for office.

SENATOR
JOHN GLENN

THE FIRST OBSTACLE to running for elected office was Glenn's commission in the U.S. Marines. Under the Hatch Act, soldiers were forbidden to express political views in public, lest they be considered a challenge to the president.

Despite the Hatch Act, Glenn entered the 1964 Senate race against Democratic incumbent Stephen Young of Ohio. Young was quick to point out that Glenn had no experience in government. To further complicate his campaign, a slip in the bathroom took Glenn off the campaign trail altogether.

Glenn with President Lyndon Johnson (far right) in 1965. Upon Glenn's retirement from the Marines, Johnson promoted him to the rank of colonel.

Glenn suffered a concussion that made him unable to walk for a time. Annie Glenn, whom he had attempted to shield from public attention because of her stutter, took over. She spoke very little, but at least she reminded voters that John Glenn was a candidate.

As the election drew near, Glenn withdrew from the race. His injuries had not healed, and there was little chance that he would be elected while recuperating in bed. "It is better to terminate these efforts now rather than carry on until the last moment with any false hopes," he said. Glenn's disappointment was even greater when he learned that he was more than $9,000 in debt from the campaign.

Private Citizen

That same year, the Marines approved Glenn's request for retirement. President Lyndon Johnson, who took over the presidency after John Kennedy was assassinated, promoted Glenn to colonel. On that high note, Glenn's military career came to an end. For the first time in his adult life, John Glenn was unemployed and in debt.

The fame of being a space traveler had brought many offers from advertisers and other businesses who wanted to use his name. Glenn turned these down, not wanting to make a profit from his fame. In 1964, however, he worked out a deal with the Royal Crown Cola Company, the third-largest soft drink company in America. The arrangement would allow him time to pursue other things and still provide a handsome salary. Crown Cola also agreed not to use Glenn for advertisements.

His position on the board of directors of Crown Cola allowed him to travel throughout the country and abroad. He thoroughly enjoyed the flexibility of his new position, which also gave him time to consult for NASA and to lecture. Glenn still longed for closer connection with the public, and he now had the time to get out there and meet people.

His friend Robert Kennedy put Glenn's skills to good use during Kennedy's 1965 campaign for the Senate and his 1968 run for president. While campaigning together in 1968, the two stopped at the Ambassador Hotel in Los Angeles for a press conference. As Kennedy moved through the corridors toward the podium, a man shot him at close range with a handgun. Glenn rushed to the hospital with his friend, but it was too late. Two Kennedy brothers had now been assassinated. Glenn was horrified by the senselessness of it.

The generally peaceful business of running for office in the United States had suddenly become a battle with actual casualties. The United States was changing quickly and Glenn felt that good and honest leadership could set things right.

Skiing with good friend Robert Kennedy (right). Glenn was present when the senator was assassinated.

Back in the Ring

Glenn's chance to serve in the U.S. Senate—a body of one hundred elected officials, two from each state—came in 1974, when the senior senator from Ohio retired. As the Senate race began to shape up, Glenn found himself once again outside the local Democratic machine, which backed his opponent, Howard Metzenbaum. Glenn reacted to the stiff-arm tactics of the Democratic Party with his characteristic fighting spirit.

When Metzenbaum accused Glenn of never holding a job, the former Marine was given the opening to stress his greatest contribution, his lifelong service to the country. "You stand in Arlington National Cemetery—where I have more friends than I like to remember," Glenn responded to Metzenbaum in a public appearance, "and you watch those waving flags and you stand there and you think about this nation, and you tell me that those people didn't have jobs."

The people of Ohio overwhelmingly agreed with Glenn, and many were deeply offended by Metzenbaum's remark. Glenn won a landslide victory in the primary and easily won the Senate seat the following November. Glenn now represented the people of

Jacqueline Kennedy, widow of President Kennedy, supported John Glenn in his political endeavors.

Ohio as their elected leader in the more powerful of the two houses of Congress.

Jacqueline Kennedy, the widow of the slain president, perhaps best summed up Glenn's appeal in a TV endorsement she made during the campaign: "John Glenn's leadership would be a shining light in the United States Senate," the wildly popular former first lady said. "I have never done anything political for anyone before, but I feel that both I and the country have an obligation to John Glenn."

A New Form of Service

In many ways, Glenn was exceptionally well suited to the Senate. Its one hundred members worked in a friendlier environment than the one felt in the much larger House of Representatives. In the Senate, members took a more problem-oriented approach to lawmaking. Glenn entered with that kind of can-do approach. "I thought I could make reasoned, principled decisions on the issues by learning the facts, keeping in close touch with my constituents [the people of Ohio], and finding a balance between their needs and those of the country as a whole," he said.

Among members of the Senate, Glenn earned a reputation for fairness. The Democrats found him to be a great asset to the party, and the Republicans found that he was a man they could work with. When Glenn approached a bill, he first mastered all the details of the issue, then worked out just what was at stake. He became an expert on scientific and technical matters, and he served on the Foreign

Relations Committee and the Committee on Energy and the Environment.

Most of the work in the Senate was done in the committees, and Glenn was happy to throw himself into foreign affairs and other intricate matters. Glenn's interest in foreign policy and his expertise on scientific matters came together in one very important aspect of the Cold War—the proliferation of nuclear weapons.

After the United States dropped atomic weapons on Japan to end World War II, other nations raced to get the superweapon. The Soviet Union now had the bomb, as did Great Britain, France, and China. Many other nations were trying to develop the bomb, either openly or in secret. "I had been through World War II and Korea and knew what happens in conventional [non-nuclear] war," Glenn wrote. "The horror of a nuclear holocaust was beyond imagining."

The fear of nuclear war with the Russians had become an everyday part of American life, and Glenn was determined to reduce that threat. In 1978, the passage of the Nuclear Non-Proliferation Act, a cornerstone of American nuclear policy, was in part the result of Glenn's efforts. Although he distrusted the Soviets, Glenn worked tirelessly to further reduce nuclear weapons through a treaty called START II. In 1980, Glenn was elected to a second Senate term, but Ronald Reagan's presidential victory tempted Glenn to make a bid for the highest office in the land—the presidency itself.

Presidential Candidate

Reagan inherited a country troubled by inflation, a weak economy, and a lack of confidence. To strengthen the economy, Reagan made massive spending cuts in government programs and created tax cuts as incentives for business growth. Glenn, like many other Democrats, disagreed with the president's approach, known as Reaganomics. It was just too hard on the people, Glenn thought.

On April 21, 1983, toward the end of Reagan's first term, Glenn announced his intention to run for president. Glenn felt he had represented the people of Ohio well and now hoped to do the same for the country.

Campaigning in New Hampshire. Glenn felt he had much to offer the American people, but was unable to win the Democratic nomination.

Glenn took moderate views in contrast to Reagan's strong conservatism. He felt that he could counter Reagan's popular hard-line approach to the Soviet Union by stressing his own record as a veteran. Before he could test this strategy though, Glenn had to win the Democratic primary.

Glenn faced Democrats Walter Mondale and Gary Hart in the race. He made a good start, raising enormous amounts of money to fund his campaign and polishing his speaking technique by hiring a speech coach and speechwriters. Even his wife, who had so dreaded public speaking, made full-length speeches on the campaign trail. (Glenn liked to introduce himself by saying, "Hello, I am Annie Glenn's husband.")

Even with coaching, Glenn wasn't an inspiring speaker. He addressed specific problems, such as nuclear weapons, but many voters found him dull and got lost in the details. As the primary results came in, Mondale took the lead. Glenn was forced to pull out of the race. In the general election, Ronald Reagan was reelected easily. Glenn later said that this was one of the greatest disappointments of his life.

Return to the Senate

In 1986, the people of Ohio sent Glenn back to the Senate for his third term as their representative. When they elected him again in 1992, Glenn

Senator Glenn served on the Senate's Special Committee on Aging, which studied health care and housing for the elderly.

became the first person from Ohio ever to be elected to a fourth term. Although he had never quite fit perfectly in the Democratic Party, that didn't seem to matter much anymore to the majority of Ohio voters. He had become the "grand old man" of Ohio politics and, indeed, United States politics.

On returning to the Senate, Glenn became interested in the elderly. He joined the Special Committee on Aging, which examined long-term options for health care and housing for the elderly and the government's role in paying for it. "I have never gotten over the shock of seeing my father's retirement nest egg consumed by the costs of his cancer treatment," Glenn wrote.

His interest in aging did not stop with the dollars and cents of insurance coverage, however. He became interested in the science of aging. How does the body change as it ages? What can be done to prolong life? What can science possibly discover through space travel to cure diseases like arthritis, which causes pain day in and day out?

NASA scientists wanted to know what effect space travel had on human faculties, such as memory, balance, heart rate, bone density, and vision. The continued use of these physical faculties or their restoration is also a concern for people who are aging. To further NASA's studies and to benefit the elderly, Glenn was inspired to return to space one final time.

"My idea was to send an older person up and study the body's reaction to space flight," he said. "I went over to NASA to talk to Dan Goldin, the administrator. I made no bones about it—I wanted to be the person to do it."

At a news conference at the National Air and Space Museum. The event marked the 25th anniversary of Glenn's orbit in space.

Back into Space

By 1998, spaceflights had become almost routine. The early space rockets had evolved into what were now called space shuttles, which looked more like planes strapped to booster rockets. The shuttles carried several astronauts along with a payload of satellites. Because the shuttles were so large, NASA was able to to use them as floating laboratories, in which hundreds of experiments could be conducted. Large computers that were also on board would then help scientists analyze data.

Goldin liked the idea and gave Glenn permission to serve as a human "lab rat" for experiments on aging and the effects of space flight on the elderly body. Glenn's announcement that he would return to space, just a year after he announced that he would not run for a fifth term in the Senate, caused a national debate both through the radio and television airwaves, as well as in the print media.

Critics accused NASA of using Glenn and the shuttle flight simply to attract increased funding for future projects. Others accused NASA of giving in to Glenn's frivolous wish—to go to space again just because he wanted to. They said that Glenn offered nothing to the space program, but was just being rewarded with one last trip as a gesture because he was already famous.

But Glenn's flight plan was approved by a panel of scientists who believed that important questions might be answered by sending an elderly man into space. The fact that Glenn was an experienced astronaut made him the perfect candidate.

The mission objectives for STS-95, space shuttle *Discovery,* included the release and retrieval of a solar observation satellite and several chemical and geological experiments. Of the seven astronauts aboard on the mission, Glenn would be the lowest in rank. "I know there was a lot of personal interest in me, but the other people on this flight were more important to the overall mission than I was," Glenn later said.

When NASA approved the mission, they assured Glenn that he would receive no special treatment or leniency when it came to training sessions. If Glenn didn't seem fit enough by the launch date, he simply wouldn't go.

Fortunately, Glenn had been one of the most physically active senators in Washington, jogging, talking long walks, and making the occasional airplane flight. For the first time since his early days at

Glenn onboard space shuttle Discovery. *The seventy-seven-year-old underwent a number of medical tests while in space.*

NASA more than thirty-six years ago, the seventy-seven-year-old astronaut climbed back into a giant centrifuge that simulated G-force pressure. Once again he was shaken, probed, X-rayed, and examined by NASA scientists.

As the launch date for space shuttle *Discovery* drew near, it became clear to everyone that the mission was going to go forward. Even Glenn's most vocal earlier critics began to wonder what would happen when a seventy-seven-year-old man was blasted out of the atmosphere. "People are thinking differently," Glenn said.

One day, Glenn received a note from Strom Thurmond, the ninety-six-year-old senator from South Carolina as well as the oldest person to ever serve in the United States Senate. "I want to go too," Thurmond wrote to his colleague.

On October 29, 1998, the shuttle *Discovery* carried John Glenn 345 miles (555 km) above Earth's surface. Once he was in space, Glenn radioed the Cape, "Zero G, and I feel fine," he said, echoing the first words he had spoken from the *Friendship 7* on February 20, 1962. The space pioneer was back in orbit.

Glenn sent an e-mail to President Bill Clinton.

Glenn with his NASA crew in 1998. Some people opposed his return to space, but many embraced the idea.

John and Annie Glenn waving to the crowds during a 1998 ticker-tape parade in New York City

"An e-mail's probably never been sent to the president of the United States from space," Glenn reasoned. "And he'd appreciate it too."

When Glenn returned to Earth more than a week later, he climbed out of the shuttle, weak and a little disoriented—but he insisted on taking a postflight walk around the shuttle with the crew members. The seasoned astronaut kept his cool on the outside but, inside, he was nearly jumping out of his skin with elation. Since then, he has more than once hinted that he would like to go up again.

John Glenn speaks to a group (including NASA director Dan Goldin, left) after returning from his shuttle mission.

TIMELINE

1921	John Glenn born in Cambridge, Ohio, on July 18
1939	Enrolls in Muskinguam College
1941	Earns pilot's license
1942	Enters the Naval Aviation Cadet Program
1943	Marries Annie Margaret Castor; enlists in the U.S. military.
1944–45	Flies 59 combat missions in World War II; wins Air Medal with 18 clusters for combat duty.
1945	Son David is born
1947	Daughter Carolyn is born
1950–53	Serves in the Korean War
1954	Becomes a Marine test pilot
1957	Sets a new record for supersonic flight
1959	Is selected by NASA as one of seven Mercury Project astronauts from an original pool of 508
1962	On February 20, is launched into space aboard the Mercury-Atlas 6, called the *Friendship 7*
1965	Retires from the Marine Corps; joins the board of directors of Royal Crown Cola

1966	Joins television series *Great Explorations*
1968	Works for Democrat Robert F. Kennedy's presidential campaign
1970	Runs for U.S. Senate but loses the Democratic primary
1972	Creates television documentary *Here Comes Tomorrow* with David Wolper
1974	Wins a seat in the U.S. Senate representing Ohio
1976	Is one of three men considered by Jimmy Carter to serve as vice president
1978	Congress passes the Nuclear Non-Proliferation Act, which Glenn had campaigned for in the Senate
1980	Is reelected to Senate
1983	Announces he will run for president
1984	Withdraws from Democratic presidential race
1986	Is elected to a third term in the U.S. Senate
1992	Is reelected to U.S. Senate, making him the first four-term U.S. Senator from Ohio
1997	Announces that he will not run for a fifth term in the Senate
1998	Ohio State University announces the creation of the John Glenn Institute for Public Service and Public Policy; returns to space aboard the shuttle *Discovery*

HOW TO BECOME AN ASTRONAUT

The Job

Astronauts conduct experiments and gather information while in spaceflight. They also experiment with the space-craft itself to develop new concepts in design, engineer ing, and the navigation of a vehicle outside Earth's atmosphere.

Astronauts are part of a complex team. Throughout the flight, they remain in contact with Mission Control and various tracking stations around the globe. Space-technology experts on the ground monitor each flight closely. Flight directors on the ground provide the astronauts with important information and help them solve any problems that arise.

The crew of a space shuttle is made up of at least five people: the commander, the pilot, and three mission specialists—all NASA astronauts. Some flights also require a payload specialist, who becomes the sixth member of the crew. From time to time, other experts are on board. Depending on the purpose of the mission, they may be engineers, technicians, physicians, or scientists such as astronomers, meteorologists, or biologists.

The commander and the pilot of a space shuttle are both pilot astronauts who know how to fly aircraft and spacecraft. Commanders are in charge of the overall mission. They fly the orbiter, supervise the crew and the operation of the vehicle, and are responsible for the success and safety of the flight. Pilots help the commanders control and operate the orbiter and may help manipulate satellites by using a remote control.

Mission specialists, also trained astronauts, work with the commander and the pilot. Mission specialists work on specific experiments, perform tasks outside the orbiter, and use remote-manipulator systems to handle payloads. One or more payload specialists may be included on a flight. A payload specialist may not be a NASA astronaut but is always an expert on the cargo being carried into space.

Although much of their work is done in space, astronauts do a great deal of groundwork before and during launching. Just prior to liftoff, they go through checklists to be sure nothing has been forgotten. When the rocket boosters are used up and the external fuel tank is empty, they break away from the orbiter. Once in orbit, the astronauts take control of the craft. They can change its position or course or maneuver it into position with other vehicles.

Another important part of an astronaut's work is the deployment of satellites. Communications satellites transmit telephone calls, TV programs, educational and medical information, and emergency instructions. Some satellites are used to observe and predict weather, and chart ocean currents and tides. Others measure Earth's various surfaces and check its natural resources.

Astronauts are trained in all aspects of space flight. Laboratory work is done in spaceflight simulators, which duplicate many of the characteristics of spaceflight. To ensure their safety, astronauts learn to adjust to changes in air pressure and extreme heat and take careful note their physical and psychological reactions to these changes. They must be prepared to respond to a variety of circumstances.

Requirements

High School High-school students interested in a career as an astronaut should follow a college preparatory curriculum in high school, with as much work in mathematics and science as possible. Preparing to get into a good college is important, because NASA considers the quality of a college program when accepting astronaut candidates. Earning the best possible scores on standardized tests, such as the ACT or SAT, helps you get into a good college program. NASA contributes funds to fifty-one colleges and universities. By attending one of these institutions, you are assured that the curriculum for the space programs offered will meet NASA guidelines. To receive a list of these schools, write to: NASA Education Division, Code FEO2, 300 E Street, S.W., Washington, DC 20546.

Postsecondary Any adult in excellent physical condition who meets the basic qualifications may be selected for astronaut training, according to NASA. The basic requirements are U.S. citizenship and a minimum of a bachelor's degree in engineering, biological or physical science, or mathematics. There is no age limit, but all candidates must pass the NASA spaceflight physical. Beyond these basic requirements, there may be additional requirements, depending on the astronaut's role. NASA specifies additional requirements for two other types of astronaut—the mission specialist and the pilot astronaut.

Mission specialists must have at least a bachelor's degree in one of the four areas of specialty—engineering, biological science, physical science, or mathematics—but graduate degrees are preferred. In addition, candidates must have at least three years of related work experience. Advanced degrees can take the place of part or all of the work experience requirements. Mission specialists must pass a NASA Class II physical, which includes the following standards: 20/200 or better distance visual acuity, correctable to 20/20 in each eye; blood pressure no higher than 140 over 90; and height between 58.5 and 76 inches (147 and 193 centimeters).

A pilot-astronaut candidate must meet three major requirements. A bachelor's degree in one of the four areas of specialty is required; an advanced degree is desirable. Candidates must have at least 1,000 hours of pilot-in-command time in jet aircraft. Pilot astronauts must also pass a physical, with 20/70 or better distance visual acuity, correctable to 20/20 in each eye; blood pressure no higher than 140 over 90; and height between 64 and 76 inches (162 and 193 cm). Because of the flight-time requirement, most pilot astronauts come from the military.

Other Requirements Astronauts must be highly trained, skilled professionals with a tremendous desire to learn about outer space and to participate in its extremely dangerous exploration. They must have a deep curiosity with extremely fine and quick reactions. They may have to react in emergency conditions that they have never before experienced, so they must be able to remain calm and think quickly and logically. As individuals, they must also be able to respond intelligently to strange and unusual conditions and circumstances.

Exploring

Students who wish to become astronauts may find it helpful to write to organizations concerned with space-flights. Many books are available on space exploration, both in your school library and your city library. In a NASA Web publication, called *Space Academy*, Colonel Charlie Bolden, of the U.S. Naval Academy, advises students to read everything they can find about astronauts and space in general.

Space camps for high-school and older students are all over the nation. These camps are not owned or operated by NASA, so the quality of their programs may vary greatly. Your high-school counselor can help you find more information on space camps in your area.

Employers

All active astronauts are employed by NASA, although some payload specialists may also be employed else-where, such as by a university or private company. All are NASA-trained and paid. Within the NASA program, astro-nauts may be classified as civil-service employees or military personnel, depending on their background. Astro-nauts who gain astronaut status through their military branch remain members of that military branch and maintain their rank. Astronauts who go to college and test into the program are civil-service employees.

Starting Out

You can begin laying the groundwork toward making your astronaut application stand out from others when you are in college. Successful astronauts have distinguished themselves from the hundreds of other applicants by gaining practical experience. Internships and work/study positions in your area of interest are a good way to gain vital experience. Your college-placement office can help direct you to such opportunities. Working in a lab on campus as a teacher assistant or research assistant in a lab is another good way to make yourself more marketable later on.

When other qualifications are met, a student applies to become an astronaut by requesting and filling out U.S. Government Application Form 171 from NASA, Johnson Space Center, ATTN: Astronaut Selection Office, Houston, TX 77058, 281-483-5907. The form is reviewed at the Johnson Space Center, where all astronauts train. The application will be ranked according to your height, experience, and expertise. Active-duty military applicants do not apply to NASA. Instead, they submit applications to their own military branch. Entrance is competitive. Aspiring astronauts compete with an average of 4,014 applicants for an average of 20 slots that open up every two years, according to NASA. From the pool of 4,014 applicants, about 118 are asked to come to the Johnson Space Center for a week of interviews and medical examinations and orientation. Then, the Astronaut Selection Board interviews applicants and assigns them a rating. Those ratings are passed on to a NASA administrator, who makes the final decision.

Entrance into the profession involves extensive piloting or scientific experience. Those hoping to qualify as pilot astronauts are encouraged to gain experience in all kinds of flying. They should consider military service and attempt to gain experience as a test pilot. People interested in becoming mission-specialist astronauts should earn at least one advanced degree and gain experience in one or more of the accepted fields, such as engineering, biological or physical science, and mathematics.

Advancement

Advancement is not a formal procedure. Astronauts who are members of the military generally rise in rank when they become astronauts and as they gain experience. Those employed by the civil service may rise from the GS-11 to GS-14 rating. Those who gain experience as astronauts will probably work in positions of management when they retire from actual flight status. Some astronauts direct future space programs or head space laboratories or factories. Some astronauts return to military service and continue to rise in rank. As recognized public figures, astronauts can enter elected office and enjoy government and public-speaking careers.

Work Environment

The work of an astronaut is difficult, challenging, and potentially dangerous. Astronauts work closely as a team because their safety depends on it. They work a normal 40-hour week when preparing and testing for a spaceflight but, as countdown approaches and activity is stepped up, they may work long hours, seven days a week. While on a mission, of course, they work as many hours as necessary to accomplish their objectives.

The training period is rigorous, and conditions in the simulators and trainers can be restrictive and uncomfortable. Exercises to produce the effect of weightlessness may cause air sickness in trainees. Astronauts on a space flight must become accustomed to floating around in cramped quarters. Because of the absence of gravity, they eat and drink either through a straw or very carefully with fork and spoon. All bathing is done with a washcloth, as there are no showers in the spacecraft. Astronauts buckle and zip themselves into sleep bunks to keep from drifting around the cabin. Sleeping is generally done in shifts, which means that lights, noises, and activity are constant.

During the launch and when working outside the spacecraft, astronauts wear specially designed space suits to protect them against various facets of the new environment.

Earnings

For most, the attraction to being an astronaut is not the salary—and with good reason. The field is one of the most rewarding, but astronauts don't receive large salaries. Astronauts begin their salaries in accordance with the U.S. government pay scale. Astronauts enter the field at a minimum classification of GS-11, which in 2000 paid a minimum of $39,178, according to the Office of Personnel Management General Schedule. As they gain experience, astronauts may advance up the classification chart to peak at GS-14, which pays between $63,567 and

$82,638. Of course, there are opportunities outside NASA (although these don't involve spaceflight) that may pay higher salaries. Astronauts who leave NASA often work for universities or private space laboratories that pay six-figure salaries.

In addition, astronauts get the usual benefits, including vacations, sick leave, health insurance, retirement pensions, and bonuses for superior performance. Salaries for astronauts who are members of the armed forces consist of base pay, an allowance for housing and subsistence, and flight pay. Earnings for astronauts employed by the military range from $46,200 to $90,250 per year.

Outlook

Only a very few people will ever be astronauts. NASA chooses its astronauts from an increasingly diverse pool of applicants. From thousands of applications sent in from all over the country, approximately 100 men and women are chosen for an astronaut training program every two years. The small number of astronauts is not likely to change in the near future. Space exploration is an expensive venture for the governments that fund it, and often the program can barely maintain its present funding levels. Large increases in funding, which would allow for more astronauts, are highly unlikely. While the international space-station project has generated increased public interest and will likely continue to do so as discoveries are reported, the project still requires that there be only six astronauts at one time aboard the station.

TO LEARN MORE ABOUT ABOUT ASTRONAUTS

Books

Baird, Anne. *The U.S. Space Camp Book of Astronauts.* New York: William Morrow, 1996.

Hopping, Lorraine Jean. *Sally Ride: Space Pioneer.* New York: McGraw-Hill, 2000.

Jeffrey, Laura S. *Christa McAuliffe: A Space Biography.* Springfield, N.J.: Enslow, 1998.

Maze, Stephanie. *I Want to Be an Astronaut.* New York: Harcourt Brace, 1997.

Naden, Corinne J. *Ronald McNair.* Broomall, Penn.: Chelsea House, 1993.

Websites

Ask an Astronaut

http://www.starport.com/live/astro/

To have your questions answered by astronauts; also includes biographies and multimedia files

Astronaut Hall of Fame
http://www.astronauts.org/home.htm
For biographies of astronauts in the hall of fame and information about field trips and space camp

National Aeronautics and Space Administration
http://www.nasa.gov
The official site of the government body that leads all space projects; provides information about becoming an astronaut as well as biographies of current astronauts

Where to Write
Astronaut Candidate Program
Mail Code AHX
NASA–Johnson Space Center
Houston, TX 77058

National Aeronautics and Space Administration
Office of Educational Programs and Services
Code XEP
Washington, DC 20546
For more information about a career as an astronaut

HOW TO BECOME A GOVERNMENT OFFICIAL

The Job

Federal and state officials hold positions in the legislative, executive, and judicial branches of government at the state and national levels. They include governors, judges, senators, representatives, and the president and vice president of the country. Government officials are responsible for preserving the government against external and domestic threats. They also supervise and resolve conflicts between private and public interests, regulate the economy, protect the political and social rights of the citizens, and provide goods and services. Officials may, among other things, pass laws, set up social-service programs, and decide how to spend the taxpayers' money.

Nearly every state's governing body resembles that of the federal government. Just as the U.S. Congress is composed of the Senate and the House of Representatives, every state except Nebraska has a senate and a house. The executive branch of the U.S. government is headed by the president and vice president, while the states elect governors and lieutenant governors. The governor is the chief executive officer of a state. In all states, a large group of officials handle agriculture, highway and motor-vehicle supervision, public safety and corrections, regulation of intrastate business and industry, and some aspects of education, public health, and welfare. The governor's job is to oversee their work. Some states also have a lieutenant governor, who serves as the presiding officer of the state's senate. Other elected officials commonly include a secretary of state, state treasurer, state auditor, attorney general, and superintendent of public instruction.

Besides the president and vice president of the United States, the executive branch of the national government consists of the president's cabinet. The cabinet includes the secretaries of state, treasury, defense, interior, agriculture, and health and human services. These officials are appointed by the president and approved by the Senate. The members of the Office of Management and Budget, the Council of Economic Advisors, and the National Security Council are also executive officers of the national government.

State senators and state representatives are elected to represent various districts and regions of cities and counties within the state. The number of members in a state's legislature varies from state to state. The U.S. Congress has 100 senators as established by the Constitution—2 senators from each state—and 435 representatives. (The number of representatives is based on a state's population—California has the highest number of representatives with 52.) The primary job of all legislators, on both the state and national levels, is to make laws.

With a staff of assistants, senators and representatives learn as much as they can about the bills being considered. They research legislation, prepare reports, meet with constituents and interest groups, speak to the press, and discuss legislation on the floor of the House or Senate. Legislators also may be involved in selecting other members of the government, supervising the government administration, gathering and spending money, impeaching executive and judicial officials, and setting up election procedures, among other activities. For example, a state legislator may examine the state's relationship to Native American groups, the level of school violence, and welfare reform.

Requirements

High School Courses in government, civics, and history will help you gain an understanding of the structure of state and federal governments. English courses are also important. You need good writing skills to communicate with your constituents and other government officials. Math and accounting will help you develop the analytical skills needed to understand statistics and demographics. Science courses will help you make decisions concerning health, medicine, and technological advances. Journalism classes will help you learn about the media and the role they play in politics.

Postsecondary State and federal legislators come from all walks of life. Some hold master's degrees and doctorates, while others have only a high-school education. Although most government officials hold law degrees, others have undergraduate or graduate degrees in such areas as journalism, economics, political science, history, and English. No matter what you majored in as an undergraduate, you'll likely be required to take classes in English literature, statistics, a foreign language, Western civilization, and economics. Graduate students concentrate more on one area of study; some prospective government officials pursue a master's degree in public administration or international affairs.

Exploring

A person as young as sixteen years old can gain experience working with the legislature. The U.S. Congress, and possibly your own state legislature, have opportunities for teenagers to work as pages. They want young people who have demonstrated a commitment to government study. If you work for Congress, you'll be running messages across Capitol Hill, and you'll have the opportunity to see senators and representatives debating and discussing bills. The length of a page's service can be from one summer to one year. Contact your state's senator or representative for an application.

Become involved with local elections. Many candidates for local and state offices welcome young people to assist with campaigns. You'll make calls, post signs, and get to see a candidate at work. You'll also meet others with an interest in government, and your experience will help you gain a more prominent role in later campaigns.

Another great way to learn about government is to become involved in an issue of interest to you. Get involved in a grassroots movement or read about the bills proposed in the state legislature and U.S. Congress. If you feel strongly about an issue and are well educated on the subject, contact the offices of state legislators and members of Congress to express your views.

Employers
State legislators work for the state government, and many hold other jobs as well. Because of the part-time nature of some legislative offices, state legislators may hold part-time jobs or own their own businesses. Federal officials work full-time for the Senate, the House, or the executive branch.

Starting Out
There is no direct career path for state and federal officials. Some stumble into their positions after some success with political activism on the grassroots level. Others work their way up from local government positions to state legislature and then into federal office. Those who serve in the U.S. Congress have worked in the military, journalism, academics, business, and many other fields.

Advancement
Initiative is one key to success in politics. Advancement can be rapid for someone who is a fast learner and is independently motivated, but a career in politics usually takes a long time to establish. Most state and federal officials start by pursuing training and work experience in their particular field, while getting involved in politics at the local level. Many people progress from local politics to state politics. It is not uncommon for a state legislator to eventually run for a seat in Congress. Appointees to the president's cabinet and presidential and vice presidential candidates frequently have held positions in Congress.

Work Environment

Most government officials work in a typical office setting. Some may work a regular 40-hour week, while others work long hours and weekends. One potential drawback to political life, particularly for the candidate running for office, is that there is no real off-duty time. The individual is continually under observation by the press and public, and the personal lives of candidates and officeholders are discussed frequently in the media.

Because these officials must be appointed or elected in order to keep their jobs, it is difficult to plan for long-range job objectives. There may be long periods of unemployment, when living off savings or working at other jobs may be necessary.

Frequent travel is involved in campaigning and in holding office. People with children may find this lifestyle demanding on their families.

Earnings

In general, salaries for government officials tend to be lower than salaries in the private sector. For state legislators, the pay can be very much lower. According to the National Conference of State Legislatures, state legislators make $10,000 to $47,000 a year. A few states, however, don't pay state legislators anything but an expense allowance. Even those legislators who receive a salary may not receive any benefits. However, a state's top officials are paid better: The *Book of the States* lists salaries of state governors as ranging from $60,000 to $130,000.

The Congressional Research Service publishes the salaries and benefits of Congress members. Senators and representatives are paid $136,673 annually. Congress members are entitled to a cost-of-living increase every year but don't always accept it. Congressional leaders such as the Speaker of the House and the Senate majority leader receive higher salaries than other Congress members. For example, the Speaker of the House makes $171,500 a year and U.S. Congress members receive excellent insurance, vacation, and other benefits.

Outlook

To attract more candidates for legislative offices, states may consider salary increases and better benefits for state senators and representatives. But changes in pay and benefits for federal officials are unlikely. An increase in the number of representatives is possible as the U.S. population grows, but it would require additional office space and other costly expansions. For the most part, the structures of state and federal legislatures will remain unchanged, although the topic of limiting the number of terms a representative is allowed to serve often arises in election years.

TO LEARN MORE ABOUT GOVERNMENT OFFICIALS

Books

Bonner, Mike. *How to Become an Elected Official.* Broomall, Penn.: Chelsea House, 2000.

Feinberg, Barbara Silberdick. *Local Governments.* New York: Franklin Watts, 1993.

Fish, Bruce, and Becky Durost Fish. *The History of the Democratic Party.* Broomall, Penn.: Chelsea House, 2000.

James. Lesley. *Women in Government: Politicians, Lawmakers, Law Enforcers.* Austin, Tex.: Raintree/Steck Vaughn, 2000.

Lutz, Norma Jean. *The History of the Republican Party.* Broomall, Penn.: Chelsea House, 2000.

Sandak, Cass R. *Congressional Committees.* New York: Twenty-First Century, 1995.

Stein, R. Conrad. *The Powers of Congress.* Chicago: Childrens Press, 1995.

Websites
Congress
http://www.congress.org/
A guide to Congress, providing information about House and Senate members as well as current bills

U.S. House of Representatives
http://www.house.gov
Provides a variety of information about the House of Representatives

U.S. Senate
http://www.senate.gov
Information about current senators and the Senate

Where to Write
U.S. Senate
Office of Senator (Name)
United States Senate
Washington, DC 20515

U.S. House of Representatives
Office of Representative (Name)
Washington, DC 20515

National Conference of State Legislatures
1560 Broadway,
Suite 700
Denver, CO 80202
For information about *State Legislatures Magazine*, and other information concerning state legislatures

TO LEARN MORE ABOUT JOHN GLENN

Books
Cole, Michael D. *Friendship 7: First American in Orbit.* Springfield, N.J.: Enslow, 1995.

Kramer, Barbara. *John Glenn: A Space Biography.* Springfield, N.J.: Enslow, 1998.

Streissguth, Tom. *John Glenn.* Minneapolis: Lerner, 1999.

Websites
Glenn Discovery Flight
http://www.glennflight.com/
A collection of articles from Ohio media covering Glenn's return to space

John Glenn, American Hero
http://www.pbs.org/kcet/johnglenn/
A site based on the PBS program of the same name

John Glenn: An American Hero
http://members.tripod.com/~johnhglenn/index.html
An article about Glenn's life

NASA: John Glenn
http://www.jsc.nasa.gov/Bios/htmlbios/glenn-j.html
The official NASA biography of Glenn

National Archives and Records Administration Online Exhibit Hall: John Glenn
http://www.nara.gov/exhall/glenn/glenn.html
A brief biography of John Glenn, photographs, and links

Interesting Places to Visit
Kennedy Space Center
Cocoa, Florida 32922
321/452-2121

NASA John H. Glenn Research Center
Lewis Park
21000 Brookpark Road
Cleveland, Ohio 44135
216/433-4000

National Air and Space Museum
Smithsonian Institution
Washington, D.C. 20560
202/357-1400

The United States Capitol
Washington, D.C. 20202
202/225-6827

INDEX

Page numbers in *italics* indicate illustrations.

ABOUT THE AUTHOR

Robert Green holds an M.A. in Journalism from New York University and a B.A. in English literature from Boston University. He has written sixteen other books, including a biography of George Bush in the Ferguson Career Biographies and biographies of Alexander the Great, Tutankhamen, Julius Caesar, Hannibal, Herod the Great, Cleopatra, and six British monarchs. He has also written a book on China for young adults and *"Vive La France":* *The French Resistance During World War II* and *Dictators of the Modern World*. He lives in New York City.